Hayner Public Library District - Alton

0   W9-AOF-169

HAYNER PUBLIC LIBRARY DISTRICT
ALTON, ILLINOIS

OVERDUES .10 PER DAY MAXIMUM FINE
COST OF BOOKS. LOST OR DAMAGED
BOOKS ADDITIONAL $5.00 SERVICE CHARGE.

HOW It's MADE

A Metal Can

Sarah Ridley

GARETH**STEVENS**

PUBLISHING

A Member of the WRC Media Family of Companies

HAYNER PUBLIC LIBRARY DISTRICT
ALTON, ILLINOIS

Please visit our web site at: **www.garethstevens.com**
For a free color catalog describing Gareth Stevens Publishing's list of high-quality books
and multimedia programs, call 1-800-542-2595 (USA) or 1-800-387-3178 (Canada).
Gareth Stevens Publishing's fax: (414) 332-3567.

Library of Congress Cataloging-in-Publication Data

Ridley, Sarah, 1963-
  A metal can / Sarah Ridley.
     p. cm. — (How it's made)
  ISBN-10: 0-8368-6702-5 — ISBN-13: 978-0-8368-6702-2 (lib. bdg.)
  1. Aluminum cans—Juvenile literature. I. Title. II. Series.
TS198.C3R53   2006
671.8—dc22   2006042297

This North American edition first published in 2007 by
Gareth Stevens Publishing
A Member of the WRC Media Family of Companies
330 West Olive Street, Suite 100
Milwaukee, WI 53212 USA

This U.S. edition copyright © 2007 by Gareth Stevens, Inc.
Original edition copyright © 2006 by Franklin Watts.
First published in Great Britain in 2006 by Franklin Watts,
338 Euston Road, London NW1 3BH, United Kingdom.

Series editor: Sarah Peutrill
Art director: Jonathan Hair
Designer: Jemima Lumley

Gareth Stevens editor: Tea Benduhn
Gareth Stevens art direction: Tammy West
Gareth Stevens graphic designer: Charlie Dahl

Photo credits: (t=top, b=bottom, l=left, r=right, c=center)
James L. Amos/CORBIS: 8tr, 26cl. Anthony Blake Photo Library/Alamy: 30tr. Nathan Benn/CORBIS: 8bl. CORBIS:
24, 27tr. Howard Davies/CORBIS: 6b, 26tl. Dynamic Graphics/Alamy: 28tr. Chris Fairclough/Franklin Watts: 29.
Goodshoot/Alamy: 25b. John van Hasselt/Sygma/CORBIS: 25t, 27cr. K. Photos/Alamy: 28b. Ray Moller/Franklin
Watts: 30b. Luc Monnet/Sygma/CORBIS: 23b. NASA: 31t. Charles O'Rear/CORBIS: 7t. Charles Rotkin/CORBIS: 9.
Paul A. Souders/CORBIS: 7b. Stockbyte Silver/Alamy: 31cr. Hugh Trefall/Alamy: 28cl. Zefa/CORBIS: 5, 30cl, 31bl.
All other photography by Alan Williams. Every effort has been made to trace the copyright holders for the photos used
in this book. The publisher apologizes, in advance, for any unintentional omissions and would be pleased to insert the
appropriate acknowledgements in any subsequent edition of this publication.

All rights reserved. No part of this book may be reproduced, stored in a retrieval system, or transmitted in any form or
by any means, electronic, mechanical, photocopying, recording, or otherwise, without the prior written permission of the
copyright holder.

Printed in the United States of America

1 2 3 4 5 6 7 8 9 10 09 08 07 06

Words that appear in the glossary are printed in
boldface type the first time they occur in the text.

j671.8
RIO

b17495350

Contents

This can is made from a metal called aluminum.

This can is made for a soft drink called fizz.

One factory makes cans for many soft drink companies. Most soft drink cans are made of aluminum. Like many metals, aluminum is found in rocks under the ground. When it is taken out of the rocks, it becomes a very useful material. Aluminum is solid at room temperature, and it can be bent into shapes easily. Before work starts, the soft drink company decides how the can will look. What will be printed on the can? What color will it be?

The soft drink company can choose from a variety of push tabs.

Why aluminum?

Aluminum is a good metal to use for making soft drink cans because it is strong, lightweight, easily bent into shape, and it does not **rust**. Liquids are heavy, so cans that are filled with liquids are easier to lift and transport to stores if they are made of a light metal. The design of all soft drink cans allows the greatest number of cans to be stacked on a supermarket shelf.

Steel is also a metal that is used to make cans for food and soft drinks. It is also easy to shape, but it will rust unless it is coated with another metal called tin. Some people call tin-coated steel cans "tin cans." Many drinks and foods are stored in steel cans — from soft drinks to soup and from fruit to fish.

Can you imagine which foods might be stored in each of these cans?

Aluminum comes from bauxite, which is a type of rock.

Bauxite is a reddish rock that comes from mines in the Caribbean, West Africa, and Australia.

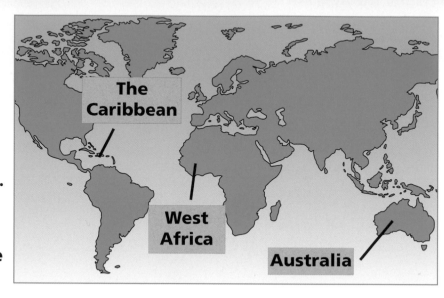

The Caribbean

West Africa

Australia

Bauxite is found in three areas of the world.

Drills or explosives break up the bauxite. Then, machines load the rocks onto trucks that take the rocks to the **processing factory.**

All the soil has to be removed before mining can begin. The mine can stretch over a huge area.

Alumina is a fine white powder.

At the processing factory, the bauxite is treated with water and chemicals until only a powder, called alumina, is left.

A substance called cryolite is added to the alumina. Strong currents of electricity pass through the mixture of alumina and cryolite, and change it into **molten** aluminum.

This red-hot aluminum will harden and turn gray as it cools.

In the Past

In 1822, Pierre Bertier discovered alumina in bauxite rocks at Les Baux in southern France. It was not until 1886, however, that chemists Charles Hall and Paul Heroult invented the process of removing alumina from bauxite. The process that Hall and Heroult invented is still used today.

Aluminum is made into ingots.

Molten aluminum is poured into molds where it hardens to form **ingots**. It takes four tons of bauxite to make one ton of aluminum ingots.

Aluminum ingots are placed in stacks.

The aluminum ingot glows yellow while it is heated.

Each aluminum ingot is 7 feet (2 meters) wide, 26 feet (8 m) long, and 2 feet (60 centimeters) thick. The factory presses each ingot into thin sheets that are still 7 feet (2 m) wide, but $\frac{1}{10}$ inch (3 millimeters) thick and very long. To make the thin sheets, the ingots are first heated to soften the metal.

Then the ingots are passed backward and forward through rollers, becoming longer and thinner each time they go through.

When the ingots become very thin sheets, they are wound onto rolls. Then they are loaded onto a truck that leaves the processing factory and travels to the can-making factory.

Huge rolls of aluminum sheets are kept in stacks at the factory.

In the Past

People have been using aluminum for only about one hundred fifty years, but other metals have been part of everyday life for thousands of years. About ten thousand years ago, people discovered that they could use fire to take metals out of particular rocks.

Over time, people experimented with different metals to make a variety of objects, from weapons to jewelry. Archaeologists have discovered some of these metal objects. Your local museum may show some of the metal objects that have been found in your area.

Rolls of aluminum arrive at the can-making factory.

The huge roll feeds into the press machine.

A can-making factory never sleeps! Its machines work all day and all night, making about six million cans per day. First, workers put a roll of sheet aluminum onto a machine called a press. The shiny sheet of aluminum feeds into the press. This sheet is coated with a thin layer of oil that makes it move smoothly through the press.

The cups stick to a conveyor belt by **suction**.

From the sheet of aluminum, the press stamps many wide, shallow dishes, called cups. The cups come out of the other end of the machine on a **conveyor belt**.

aluminum cup

Why recycle aluminum?

Millions of cans of soft drinks are opened each day across the world. Fortunately, aluminum is a great material to use for cans because it is very easy to recycle. Once it has been cleaned, it can be used over and over again. Recycling reduces the demand for new aluminum to be taken from bauxite, which leaves more in the earth for people who might need it in the future.

The side or bottom of some cans has a recycling sign like this picture.

Aluminum cups pass into the next machine.

After pressing, the aluminum cups move into the **ironing machine**, which pulls each cup into a longer shape. This process is called "ironing." At the same time as the sides are pulled, the bottom of each cup is made into a curved shape. The machine works very fast.

The cans leave the ironing machine.

The cans go back onto the conveyor belt. The next machine trims each can, with a sharp blade, to the correct size.

A conveyor belt carries cans between different machines.

The can is now a long cylinder shape.

In the Past

Before refrigerators, freezers, and cans existed, people found other ways to preserve food which could then be used at times of the year when less fresh food was available. Packing food in salt stopped it from going rotten, as did pickling food in barrels full of water, salt, and vinegar. People also hung meat and fish over smoking fires to keep them safe for eating. Many foods, such as raisins, dates, wheat, and rice were dried in the sun. People used sugar to make jam so they could taste the flavor of summer fruits in the depths of the winter. Many of these methods are still used today.

A different machine washes and rinses the cans with hot water and chemicals to remove any traces of oil. The cans then move along on a wire conveyor belt that passes through huge ovens that dry them.

Clean, dry cans leave the washing and drying machine.

The cans are decorated.

Designs are printed on cans in a decorating machine. The fizz cans are decorated with three ink colors — white, red, and yellow.

To make the design, a computer controls how much of each color is spread on a rubber blanket. Then each can rolls across the rubber blanket to pick up the ink. Next, a layer of a material called **varnish** rolls over the ink. The varnish protects the cans and gives them a shine.

A worker climbs the steps to fill the machine with red ink.

These painted cans are coming out of a drying machine.

The can has all its writing and color now.

The cans then enter a machine that dries the ink and the varnish.

The soft drink company wants to print a lot of information on the outside of the can. The strong design and colors will attract the shopper. The back shows information about the ingredients of the drink, where it was made, and how to recycle the can.

In the Past

In 1795, in France, Nicholas Appert discovered that food could be preserved by heating it in a sealed container. Then, in 1810, British merchant Peter Durand invented the metal can. At first, only about sixty cans could be made in one day, but other people began to invent faster and faster methods. Now millions of cans are made each day. It wasn't until 1935, however, that a U.S. brewer invented the flat-topped soft drink can we know today.

A machine sprays each can with lacquer.

Each can is coated on the inside with **lacquer**. The special coating keeps the metal from mixing with the contents of the can.

The cans then move into an oven that dries the lacquer.

Cans enter the lacquer machine at the top (*top left*), are sprayed, and then leave at the bottom.

At almost every stage, the machines check the cans for quality. If the cans are not quite right, they fall into the reject basket. Then they are sent back to the beginning of the process to be recycled.

Rejected cans await collection.

In the Past

Early on, some canned food was sealed with lead. Lead-sealed cans may have caused the strange disappearance of the Franklin Expedition, in 1845. Sir John Franklin set off on a voyage to discover the Northwest Passage. He took two boats and 134 men, and he made sure that the boats were carrying all the latest equipment, including about eight thousand cans of food.

When people in Britain did not hear from the expedition, they began to search for the ship and crew. The bodies of just three sailors were found, buried on an island. All had high levels of lead in their bodies, suggesting lead poisoning was the cause of their death. Some scientists now think that the lead sealant in the tin cans must have mixed with the food and entered the bodies of the sailors, eventually killing them.

The tops of the cans are formed.

This machine shapes the top of the can to form a neck.

The cans need to be made smaller at their tops to form the necks. A machine presses each can to make the neck shape. It only takes a few minutes for the can to reach this stage from its beginning as a flat sheet of aluminum. Linked together by many conveyor belts snaking across the factory, each machine has done its job.

The cans follow each other around the factory.

Why aluminum?

Lightweight, strong, and flexible, aluminum can be made even stronger by mixing it with another metal or another material. This mixture of metals is called an aluminum alloy. Different alloys are used for different purposes. Copper, for example, is added to aluminum to create an alloy called duralumin, which is used to build aircraft. Magnesium and manganese are sometimes added to the aluminum in cans to make the aluminum stronger and only very slightly heavier.

Aluminum goes from cup to almost finished can in a few minutes.

The cans get a final check.

Many cans are rejected at the final check.

The final check involves shining light through the cans. Light will show any tiny cracks or holes. The machine automatically rejects any damaged cans. All the perfect cans are packed in layers and placed on pallets. The cans are ready to be sent to the filling factory.

In the Past

Stores used to sell all drinks in glass bottles. Glass bottles are easy to clean and reuse. Glass is also easy to recycle by melting it down and starting again. Glass is heavy, however, and it breaks when dropped. Today, we can often choose whether to buy our drink in a glass bottle, a plastic bottle, or a metal can.

1. The cans go onto a wide conveyor belt. A machine packs the cans into honeycomb-like layers, which will be separated by layers of cardboard.

2. Stacks of cans arrive at a warehouse on a pallet.

3. Towering stacks of cans fill a warehouse.

4. A fork-lift driver loads the cans and takes them to a truck.

The ends of the cans are made at a different factory.

A roll of sheet aluminum feeds into a machine that stamps out thousands of can ends every minute. At the same time, the machine curls the edges and adds a sealant, which will help make the end join tightly to the can.

The aluminum sheet feeds into the end-making machine.

A finished can end needs a push tab. The ring is stamped out of a narrow strip of aluminum and attached to the end. To make the can easy to open, a line is stamped or pressed in the metal so that it will break open with pressure.

push tab   **stamped line**

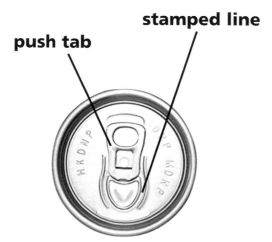

The end now looks like this.

All the ends are packed together in paper sleeves. The ends are sent to the filling factory where the soft drink will be added.

Thousands of ends are packed together in brown paper.

Opening Cans

When food cans were first invented, people had to hammer them open! Then, in 1858, the first can opener was invented, and an even better one was invented in 1870. The can opener made opening cans much easier. People could also attach a key to the top and peel back the lid of the can. In 1959, the pop-top can was invented, using a ring pull and a weakened area to literally pull an opening in the top of the can. More recently, cans have tabs that can be pushed into the can. The push tabs create less litter because there is no extra tab to throw away.

Some cans, particularly those that store fish, have a key to remove the top.

The cans and their ends arrive at the filling factory.

A huge number of cans move through the factory on conveyor belts. While the cans are waiting to be filled, it is extremely important to keep everything very clean so that no **bacteria** get inside the cans or the soft drinks.

All the workers in the soft drink factory wear hats and overalls to keep the factory clean.

First, machines clean the cans by spraying air and water on them. The next machine fills up to two thousand cans per minute with a soft drink. A final machine attaches the can ends to the filled cans.

A worker in the soft drink factory makes a final check.

To keep canned soft drinks fresh, the cans and the drinks inside are heated for long enough to kill any bacteria that might exist. To make sure the drinks will stay fresh, a code and "best before" date is printed on each can. Finally, the soft drink cans are ready to be packed and sold to stores.

These used cans can be recycled and reformed so they can be used again.

Food poisoning!

Unfortunately, in the past, canned food has been known to kill. If the food inside the cans isn't heated for long enough at the correct temperature, it is possible for deadly bacteria to survive inside. When this happens, the people who eat the food get terrible food poisoning, which can lead to death. Food poisoning is very rare today.

How a Metal Can Is Made

1. Bauxite, containing alumina, is dug out of the ground.

2. At a processing factory, machines take alumina out of bauxite and turn it into aluminum ingots.

3. Machines roll the ingots into long sheets of aluminum.

4. At the can-making factory, a press machine stamps out aluminum cups.

5. The cups pass through a machine that stretches the sides to form a can shape.

fizz

6. After a thorough cleaning, the cans are printed with a design and dried. Spray guns coat the cans with varnish.

9. The can ends are made at a different factory.

10. The cans and ends arrive at the filling factory where the cans are filled with drink and closed.

8. The cans are stored in a warehouse until they are needed.

11. The cans are heated to kill any bacteria. Each can is checked.

7. The next machine shapes the neck of each can.

12. The soft drink cans are put onto trucks, sold to stores, and bought by customers.

Metal Cans and Their Many Uses

Huge numbers of aluminum and steel cans are made each year. Cans are also put to other uses.

"Tin" cans are used to store baked beans, tuna fish, pet food, and all types of fruit and vegetables in water or syrup.

Tennis balls are sold in air-tight cans. The sealed cans help to keep the balls bouncy.

Some medicines and beauty products, such as hairspray and deodorant, are sold in cans.

Many household products, including paint, and cleaning products are sold in cans.

Recycling Aluminum

Up to half of all the aluminum in use today will be recycled. Aluminum is very easy to recycle and use over and over again. Recyclable aluminum includes cans, food packaging, foil, and the aluminum in cars, trucks, and airplanes.

Aluminum cans can be taken to a recycling center.

Reasons to Recycle Aluminum

1. Mining bauxite leaves huge scars in the landscape. Many animals, plants, and insects die, even though some mining companies use the original soil to try to restore the landscape when the mining is finished.

2. Taking aluminum out of bauxite is difficult and uses a lot of energy. Recycling existing aluminum means much less energy is used, which cuts down on the production of harmful greenhouse gases.

3. Finally, keeping aluminum cans out of your other trash reduces the amount of waste that ends up in landfill sites.

You can help by recycling all aluminum packaging. Wash out the cans or foil and place them in a box or bag for collection. In some places, you will need to take your aluminum to a recycling center.

Sometimes, it is important to separate steel and aluminum cans. Steel cans stick to a magnet while aluminum cans do not. Use a magnet to sort your cans.

Other Uses for Aluminum

Aluminum is used to make huge numbers of drink cans. Aluminum is strong and light, so it is also a suitable material for many other uses.

The lids of yogurt containers are often made of aluminum, as are many take-out or ready-to-cook meal containers.

Aluminum can be rolled into extremely thin sheets, called foil, to wrap around food to keep it fresh. Cooks also use foil to seal food that is cooking.

Heat passes through aluminum easily, making it a good material for pots and pans. The fact that it is a light metal also makes it attractive for large pans that could become very heavy.

Aluminum is used to build space rockets. These rockets need to be extremely strong but also as light as possible so less fuel is needed to launch them into space, which saves money.

Aluminum can be made into wire. Aluminum wire is used in many ways, including in cables and even to wrap the gut strings of violins.

Aluminum is a useful material for window frames that will get wet. Aluminum does not rust, unlike metals such as steel and iron.

Glossary

bacteria – the name for many different types of small, single-celled living things that live everywhere. Many bacteria are harmless, but some make us ill if they get inside our bodies.

conveyor belt – a moving belt or flat surface used to transport goods or objects around a factory

ingots – bars of solid metal

ironing machine – a machine that pulls aluminum cups into a cylinder shape

lacquer – a liquid similar to paint that dries and is used to coat metal or wood

landfill sites – huge holes in the ground used for storing waste

molten – describes a material that is so hot that it has melted into a runny liquid

processing factory – a factory where the rock bauxite is crushed, heated, and mixed with chemicals to extract aluminum from the rock

rust – to become coated with a reddish-brown substance after coming in contact with air and moisture. This rust makes the metal weaker.

suction – the act of sucking all the air out of a space. This process can make cups stick to a conveyor belt, even though they are on their sides.

varnish – a substance similar to lacquer

Index